After-School Fun

By Eliza Webb

Contents

After-School Fun

When school is finished for the day, kids can do lots of fun things with their free time.

Games Fun

Charlotte loves to play charades after school.

In charades you act out words, but you cannot talk.

If her friends all call out at once, it's chaos!

Musical Fun

Palmer is in a choir.
Singing brings her so much joy.

Today, the choir is learning to sing the chorus of a new song.

Singing with other people is called choral singing.
It sounds beautiful!

If the choir sings loud enough, it makes an echo in the big hall.

Gail loves music, too.
Twice a week, she takes music lessons after school with her sister, Tam.

Gail plays chords while Tam strums.

They are like a mini orchestra!

Tonight, Gail's grandma and grandpa are coming over for dinner.

After dinner, Gail and Tam put on a show for their family.

The family claps for the mini orchestra.

Craft Club Fun

At craft club, Lochlan builds a model volcano.

He uses glue, paint and tough paper to make the model.

Miss Christy helps him tip chemicals into the top.

The chemicals are baking soda and vinegar.

The chemicals make the volcano erupt!

Chantel makes a flower chain for her mum.

She threads orchids on string. She must not be rough with the orchids.

Kitchen Fun

Zach wants to be a chef one day, so he likes to cook meals and bake treats after school.

Today, he is making muffins.

Zach's mum and his sister, Mia, help if he needs it.

He stirs the mix well.
His arm used to ache when he had to stir a lot, but his arm got stronger!

Mia wants to drink fresh juice with her muffin, so Zach gets the juicer.

Mum slices some fruit and helps him feed the slices into the chute at the top.

Then the juice comes out the tap at the bottom!

Which fun pastime would **you** like to do after school?

CHECKING FOR MEANING

1. What is choral singing? *(Literal)*
2. Who does Chantel make a flower chain for? *(Literal)*
3. Why do you think Miss Christy helped Lochlan with the volcano? *(Inferential)*
4. Do any of the activities in the text seem like fun to you? What other activities could the author have included? *(Evaluative)*

EXTENDING VOCABULARY

chaos	What does the word *chaos* mean? Why might there be chaos if all the kids call out at once?
chemicals	Chemicals are materials that create a change in another thing. What chemicals does Lochlan use in the text? What other chemicals do you know?
chute	What is a chute used for? Is a chute hollow or solid? Why? Where might you find a chute?

MOVING BEYOND THE TEXT

1. What do you do after school? Do you do any of the activities from the text? Are there any activities that you would like to do?
2. An orchestra includes instruments with strings. Name some instruments that have strings.
3. What would you make if you went to a craft club?
4. Have you ever baked anything? What did you bake? What would you like to bake?

TIME TO WRITE

Write about an activity that you do after school, or an activity you would like to try.